Is THAT It?

A Beginner's Guide
to Navigating
the Christian Life

Neville Wheeler

Copyright © 2019 Neville Wheeler

All rights reserved.

The author has asserted the moral right to be identified as the author of this work.

All rights reserved. No part of this publication may be reproduced, stored in a retrieval system, or transmitted in any form or by any means—electronic, mechanical, photocopying, recording, or otherwise—without prior permission from the author or publisher.

Published by:
Perissos Media
www.PerissosMedia.com

(Visit us for a free guide to publishing your own books and other media)

ISBN-13: 9781696445252

Contact the author:

If you have any questions or comments for Neville, or if you want to get information on his other powerful resources, please contact him directly:

Neville Wheeler
maplit2018@gmail.com

Contents

Introduction 1
Am I a Christian or Not? 2
What Happens Now? 18
Father, Spirit, Son – What's That All About? 41
Forgiveness – Can I Keep On Sinning Then? 46
Worship, Praise and Prayer 50
What's All This Tongues Business About? 56
Denominations and "*Demon*inations" 65
I Thought Life Was Meant to Get Easier 76
Bigots, Judges and the Self-righteous 83
So Where is God When It Hurts and Why Does He Allow Suffering? 90
Next Steps 103
About the Author 105

Introduction

(…or the bit that everyone ignores!)

Making the decision to follow Jesus (to be a Christian) is to make a choice to step into the realm of spiritual warfare. It is also the best decision anyone can ever make. If you have decided to follow Christ then you need to be prepared for an amazing rollercoaster life.

One thing you will find as a Christian is that lots of people will come to you full of advice and quick to tell you what to avoid, what to read and why they are the sole holder of all that is correct and proper.

In this series of studies, we are not going to go through the basics of the Christian faith step by step but we will look at some of the areas of Christian living that can cause confusion and difficulty for the new believer.

We are not going to tell you who is right and who is wrong, as in most cases there is not a right and wrong except in condemning others for doing it differently to your preferred way. So let's get started….

Am I a Christian or Not?

It seems an odd thing to ask but many of us go through a time of questioning if it is all real or if we are play acting or if we have done everything correctly.

Sometimes it is a question in our own minds and other times it can be an accusation thrown at us by others. Sometimes those people are within our own church and some are not in any church.

We may ask ourselves if we are real because

- We just don't feel it today
- We don't feel we fit the mould of a Christian
- We don't feel forgiven
- We keep on falling back into old behaviours
- There are things from other Christians we hear that we just can't agree with.

Others may suggest we are not real because

- We have questions or doubts
- We go to a church they disagree with

- We believe something that they say is false doctrine
- We have not prayed the correct prayer.
- We have a behaviour that is incompatible with Christianity in their eyes or
- We have done something that cannot or has not been forgiven.

There are many other things that may cause us to question if we are genuine in our faith or if we have done enough to consider ourselves worthy of the title Christian. So let's start with the very basic questions.

Saved/Born Again/ Christian – what do they mean?

People use a number of phrases to describe the belief or condition that we have come to know commonly as being a Christian. People who followed Christ and acknowledged him as their Saviour and Lord of their lives were originally referred to as "Followers of the way".

The term Christian was an insult meaning "Little Christs" and was coined in Antioch where many Followers of the Way fled following persecution. We could get bogged down in the history of this town as it has been identified as being in Syria, Greece and Turkey and comprised of both Jews and

Gentiles alike. For now though let's just acknowledge that the Christian faith is one that is international and fully inclusive of all who follow Christ's teachings.

People follow the Christian faith for a number of reasons. These may dictate how we see the decision to follow Christ. Let's take a few minutes to ask ourselves the question – why do I call myself a Christian.

Is it because –

- I don't want to go to hell
- I want to change my ways
- I want to change the life I have been living
- I want emotional or spiritual healing
- I want to be part of something where I am accepted
- I want to be somewhere where I will get noticed
- I recognised my sinful condition and came to Christ
- I recognise what Christ has done for me and I worship him for it
- I recognise my life is out of control and want Christ to put it right for me
- I recognise my life is out of control and give it over to Christ to do with as he pleases

I am not saying any of these reasons are right or wrong. The truth is that probably all of us came to follow the Christian faith because it offered something better to us than what we were currently going through and after asking what's in it for me? When we found the answer we decided it was "worth it".

Speaking personally, I had a strong church based childhood but it was after meeting a variety of Christians and then hearing a particularly powerful testimony from someone whose life had been transformed that I thought "I want a piece of that life".

I had prayed some desperate prayers in difficult times and seeing how God had worked his power in those situations and now this person had shown me how he had had some miraculous interventions and healings of past hurts that I wanted more of it.

The great thing is that whatever the reason we choose to follow Christ whether that is a natural progression of our life or the result of being plucked out of the deepest septic tank of sin and depravity.

We are all accepted and loved the same by God and receive the gift of salvation. We all have to make the choice though to "be a Christian"

The Choice

Okay here we have to be careful. Does Christ reveal himself to us or do we choose Christ. If Christ reveals himself to us does that mean that he deliberately conceals himself from others and condemns them to an eternity in hell just because he can do that.

If it is a choice does that then mean that I can change my mind and then change it back again as often as I want to? Whatever our view it will give us more questions than answers.

Let's take a look at some bible teaching:.

John 3:1-21 Holman Christian Standard Bible (HCSB)

Jesus and Nicodemus
3 There was a man from the Pharisees named Nicodemus, a ruler of the Jews. ² This man came to Him at night and said, "Rabbi, we know that You have come from God as a teacher, for no one could perform these signs You do unless God were with him."
³ Jesus replied, "I assure you: Unless someone is born again,[a] he cannot see the kingdom of God."
⁴ "But how can anyone be born when he is old?" Nicodemus asked Him. "Can he enter his mother's womb a second time and be born?"
⁵ Jesus answered, "I assure you: Unless someone is born of water and the Spirit,[b] he cannot enter

the kingdom of God. [6] Whatever is born of the flesh is flesh, and whatever is born of the Spirit is spirit. [7] Do not be amazed that I told you that you[c] must be born again. [8] The wind[d] blows where it pleases, and you hear its sound, but you don't know where it comes from or where it is going. So it is with everyone born of the Spirit."

[9] "How can these things be?" asked Nicodemus.

[10] "Are you a teacher[e] of Israel and don't know these things?" Jesus replied. [11] "I assure you: We speak what We know and We testify to what We have seen, but you[f] do not accept Our testimony.[g] [12] If I have told you about things that happen on earth and you don't believe, how will you believe if I tell you about things of heaven? [13] No one has ascended into heaven except the One who descended from heaven—the Son of Man.[h] [14] Just as Moses lifted up the snake in the wilderness, so the Son of Man must be lifted up, [15] so that everyone who believes in Him will[i] have eternal life.

[16] "For God loved the world in this way:[j] He gave His One and Only Son, so that everyone who believes in Him will not perish but have eternal life. [17] For God did not send His Son into the world that He might condemn the world, but that the world might be saved through Him. [18] Anyone who believes in Him is not condemned, but anyone who does not believe is already condemned, because he has not believed in the name of the One and Only Son of God.

[19] "This, then, is the judgment: The light has come into the world, and people loved darkness rather

than the light because their deeds were evil. [20] For everyone who practices wicked things hates the light and avoids it,[k] so that his deeds may not be exposed. [21] But anyone who lives by[l] the truth comes to the light, so that his works may be shown to be accomplished by God."[m]

When Jesus meets Nicodemus, Nicodemus is willing to acknowledge that Jesus is with God. Jesus responds by telling Nicodemus that to "see the Kingdom of God" a person must be born again.

When asked what this means Jesus replies that we must be born of both water and spirit. Later in the same chapter Jesus tells the disciples that "whoever believes in him will have eternal life."

Mark 10:13-16 Holman Christian Standard Bible (HCSB)

Blessing the Children
[13] Some people were bringing little children to Him so He might touch them, but His disciples rebuked them. [14] When Jesus saw it, He was indignant and said to them, "Let the little children come to Me. Don't stop them, for the kingdom of God belongs to such as these. [15] I assure you: Whoever does not welcome[a] the kingdom of God like a little child will never enter it." [16] After taking them in His arms, He laid His hands on them and blessed them.

In this next reading we see that Jesus tells us to

come to him and to welcome the Kingdom of God like a little child.

So we are to believe in him and welcome him like a child. Let us go on further then.

Mark 10:17-25 Holman Christian Standard Bible (HCSB)

The Rich Young Ruler
[17] As He was setting out on a journey, a man ran up, knelt down before Him, and asked Him, "Good Teacher, what must I do to inherit eternal life?"
[18] "Why do you call Me good?" Jesus asked him. "No one is good but One—God. [19] You know the commandments:
Do not murder; do not commit adultery; do not steal; do not bear false witness; do not defraud; honour your father and mother."[a]
[20] He said to Him, "Teacher, I have kept all these from my youth."
[21] Then, looking at him, Jesus loved him and said to him, "You lack one thing: Go, sell all you have and give to the poor, and you will have treasure in heaven. Then come,[b] follow Me." [22] But he was stunned[c] at this demand, and he went away grieving, because he had many possessions.
Possessions and the Kingdom
[23] Jesus looked around and said to His disciples, "How hard it is for those who have wealth to enter the kingdom of God!" [24] But the disciples were astonished at His words. Again

Jesus said to them, "Children, how hard it is[d] to enter the kingdom of God! [25] It is easier for a camel to go through the eye of a needle than for a rich person to enter the kingdom of God."

One of the greatest errors in studying the bible is to only read a piece at a time or only concentrate on a small part. Nowhere have I seen this done so desperately badly as in this reading. The young man has asked Jesus – "what must I do to inherit eternal life?"

This is the same question as "what must I do to become a Christian?" remember the term Christian had not been invented at this point. Christ's response is the often understated or misquoted part of this reading.

Jesus replies by asking him about the Ten Commandments and the young man replies that he has kept all the commands since his youth which in itself is highly unlikely. Jesus then tells him

"Go sell all your possessions and give to the poor" then he adds the bit that gets missed of or overlooked "and follow me" These last three word are the ones that matter more than the others.

Keeping the law and getting rid of material wealth so as to give to the poor account for nothing if we do not follow Christ. Obedience to the law, selling our possessions and giving to the poor are what follow us following Christ, they are not a substitute for following Christ.

So we are to believe in him, welcome him like a child and follow him.

We read more in the letters that follow the gospels.

Acts 16:30-34 Holman Christian Standard Bible (HCSB)

[30] Then he escorted them out and said, "Sirs, what must I do to be saved?"
[31] So they said, "<u>Believe on the Lord Jesus, and you will be saved—you and your household.</u>" [32] Then they spoke the message of the Lord to him along with everyone in his house. [33] He took them the same hour of the night and washed their wounds. Right away he and all his family were baptized. [34] He brought them into his house, set a meal before them, and rejoiced because he had believed God with his entire household.

Romans 10:9-10 Holman Christian Standard Bible (HCSB)

[9] <u>If you confess with your mouth, "Jesus is Lord," and believe in your heart that God raised Him from the dead, you will be saved.</u> [10] One believes with the heart, resulting in righteousness,

and one confesses with the mouth, resulting in salvation.

1 Corinthians 15:1-4 Holman Christian Standard Bible (HCSB)

Resurrection Essential to the Gospel
15 Now brothers, <u>I want to clarify[a] for you the gospel I proclaimed to you; you received it and have taken your stand on it.</u> ² <u>You are also saved by it,</u> if you hold to the message I proclaimed to you—unless you believed for no purpose.[b] ³ For I passed on to you as most important what I also received:
that Christ died for our sins according to the Scriptures, ⁴ that He was buried, that He was raised on the third day according to the Scriptures.

Romans 10:13 Holman Christian Standard Bible (HCSB)

¹³ <u>For everyone who calls on the name of the Lord will be saved.[a]</u>

Acts 2:21 Holman Christian Standard Bible (HCSB)
²¹ <u>Then everyone who calls on the name of the Lord will be saved.[a]</u>

1 Corinthians 1:2-4 Holman Christian Standard Bible (HCSB)

² To God's church at Corinth, to <u>those who are</u>

sanctified in Christ Jesus and called as saints, with all those in every place who call on the nameof Jesus Christ our Lord—both their Lord and ours.
³ Grace to you and peace from God our Father and the Lord Jesus Christ.
Thanksgiving
⁴ I always thank my God for you because of God's grace given to you in Christ Jesus,

Here we come across two more statements (or is it three)

Believe in your heart and

Confess with your mouth that Jesus is Lord

Call on the name of the Lord.

We may have come to Christ for a reason other than salvation such as physical or emotional healing or simply dissatisfaction with life in general but the guaranteed result of the choice we make is that we will receive salvation and the promise of eternal life with Jesus Christ.

You may have heard what is referred to as the sinner's prayer and even seen a number of examples of it in pamphlets, books and tracts.

So we:

- are to believe in him,
- welcome him like a child

- Follow him.
- .Believe in our heart and
- Confess with our mouth that Jesus is Lord and
- Call on the name of the Lord.

Just to add a little something into the mix consider this.

Matthew 7:21-23 Holman Christian Standard Bible (HCSB)

²¹ "Not everyone who says to Me, 'Lord, Lord!' will enter the kingdom of heaven, but only the one who does the will of My Father in heaven. ²² On that day many will say to Me, 'Lord, Lord, didn't we prophesy in Your name, drive out demons in Your name, and do many miracles in Your name?' ²³ Then I will announce to them, 'I never knew you! Depart from Me, you lawbreakers!'

Notice there is a difference in the wording. The teachers say those who call on the name of the Lord whilst Jesus refers to those who call him Lord. Jesus states in this last reading that only those who do the will of the father will enter heaven. So how does that equate with all the other statements. It is actually quite straight forward if we take the time to consider it.

Let's start with "call on the name of the Lord" as

opposed to "who calls me Lord, Lord"

When I was once a rebellious teenager I had a particular manager who it was hard for me to get on with. One of the issues was that he had once been in the Royal Navy and even though he had left many years before he insisted that everyone addressed him as captain.

I, out of teenage rebellion, would always refer to him by his first name. For the most part he was unable to deal with this "insubordination" because it was a bit new to him but when I pushed the right (or should that be wrong) buttons he would get angry and shout a lot before telling me that I was to address him as captain.

Often times I would then do this. The truth was with my mouth I was saying captain but my brain was calling him something very different. We are all able to do this. We are trained in it, in many careers. Without wishing to be disrespectful to anyone or any chosen career do we really believe that the sales assistant who wishes us a lovely day actually cares about how the rest of our day goes?

At other times we hear people address customers as sir or madam. We don't actually believe or mean it but we use the words. Likewise we may be calling Jesus Lord but is that just a word or do we call on the name of the Lord acknowledging him as Lord.

- When I have a dog and it runs of I may call its name and it comes back to me
- If I run out of sugar I may call into the shop to get a fresh bag
- When I am waiting for a delivery and it does not arrive I may call the company to enquire as to where it is.
- If I am very unwell the on-call doctor may call round to visit
- When I am near friends I may call on them.

What we see here is that Jesus states that anyone can use the word Lord but not mean it. In desperation they may use the word lord but not mean that he is Lord of their life. The letters of Paul that state all who call on the name of the Lord refers to an active demonstration of being genuine in that reference.

The person who calls on the name of the Lord has actually made a choice to make Jesus Christ Lord of their life. They have then done something about it.

Am I saved then?

If you have made a decision to turn from your old way of life and have asked Jesus Christ to be Lord of your life and actually mean it then yes you are saved.

Turning from our old way of life means that we

acknowledge that the things we did in the past were wrong and that we need to power of Christ in our lives to live according to his will. We will specifically make choices to stop some things that we were doing wrong and find that other things hold no appeal to us any longer.

The fact that we will still do some stuff that others or even we feel is wrong suggests we are a work in progress it doesn't mean we are not a Christian (or not saved).

What Happens Now?

OK so you have made the choice to ask Jesus Christ to be Lord and saviour of your life, what do you do about it next?

The first thing you need to do is become part of a fellowship (Church).

Acts 2 tells us:

Acts 2:42-47 English Standard Version (ESV)

The Fellowship of the Believers
42 And they devoted themselves to the apostles' teaching and the fellowship, to the breaking of bread and the prayers. 43 And awe[a] came upon every soul, and many wonders and signs were being done through the apostles. 44 And all who believed were together and had all things in common. 45 And they were selling their possessions and belongings and distributing the proceeds to all, as any had need.
46 And day by day, attending the temple together and breaking bread in their homes, they received their food with glad and generous hearts, 47 praising God and having favour with all the people. And the Lord added to their number day by day those who were being saved.

Paul tells us in his letter to the Hebrews:

Hebrews 10:24-25 English Standard Version (ESV)

²⁴ And let us consider how to stir up one another to love and good works, ²⁵ not neglecting to meet together, as is the habit of some, but encouraging one another, and all the more as you see the Day drawing near.

And in his letter to the Colossians:

Colossians 3:16 English Standard Version (ESV)

¹⁶ Let the word of Christ dwell in you richly, teaching and admonishing one another in all wisdom, singing psalms and hymns and spiritual songs, with thankfulness in your hearts to God.

And again in the letter to the Church at Ephesus

Ephesians 4:11-13 English Standard Version (ESV)

¹¹ And he gave the apostles, the prophets, the evangelists, the shepherds[a] and teachers,[b] ¹² to equip the saints for the work of ministry, for building up the body of Christ, ¹³ until we all attain to the unity of the faith and of the knowledge of the Son of God, to mature manhood,[c] to the measure of the stature of the fullness of Christ,

I have heard a number of people ask the question "Do I need to go to church to be a Christian?" and I have heard many more people say "Of course I am a Christian – I go to church"

This opens up a wide discussion. Going to church does not make you a Christian but you need to go to church as a Christian.

Let's start with understanding what church is.

What is Church?

Ask most people to draw a church or describe church and you will get a variety of descriptions of buildings. Most of them will have a spire or steeple, some spires will be tall and majestic and others will be nominal . The insides will vary from grand gothic structures to plain modern building with either chairs or long wooden benches (pews).

Neither description is actually accurate. Church comes from the word Ekklesia which means assembly. Church is made up of people not buildings.

Church can be anywhere where Christians gather together, share, learn, teach, pray AND (not or) worship Christ. Church however cannot be on the internet or social media. This is a fallacy. It is not keeping up with the times. Jesus has made it clear what the church is and this is backed up in scripture.

Acts 2:42-47 English Standard Version (ESV)

The Fellowship of the Believers

[42] And they devoted themselves to the apostles' teaching and <u>the fellowship, to the breaking of bread and the prayers.</u> [43] And awe[a] came upon every soul, and many wonders and signs were being done through the apostles. [44] And <u>all who believed were together and had all things in common.</u> [45] And they were selling their possessions and belongings and distributing the proceeds to all, as any had need. [46] And <u>day by day, attending the temple together and breaking bread in their homes, they received their food with glad and generous hearts,</u> [47] praising God and having favour with all the people. And the Lord added to their number day by day those who were being saved.

Further on in the bible we learn that church (the fellowship of believers) serves to:

- Encourage
- Disciple
- Challenge
- Care
- Comfort

Being a part of a church (in the most local sense of the word) involves being in close communion with a group of believers' and being accountable to one another. It may upset some people. It certainly upset me but we need to come under the authority of a leadership and their agents. This again is biblical. (Eph. 4:11; 1 Tim. 3:2; 5:17; Titus 1:9; Heb. 13:17).

Let's go back to Acts for a moment.

Acts 6:1-6 English Standard Version (ESV)

Seven Chosen to Serve
6 Now in these days when the disciples were increasing in number, a complaint by the Hellenists[a] arose against the Hebrews because their widows were being neglected in the daily distribution. ² And the twelve summoned the full number of the disciples and said, "It is not right that we should give up preaching the word of God to serve tables.³ Therefore, brothers,[b] pick out from among you seven men of good repute, full of the Spirit and of wisdom, whom we will appoint to this duty. ⁴ But we will devote ourselves to prayer and to the ministry of the word." ⁵ And what they said pleased the whole gathering, and they chose Stephen, a man full of faith and of the Holy Spirit, and Philip, and Prochorus, and Nicanor, and Timon, and Parmenas, and Nicolaus, a proselyte of Antioch. ⁶ These they set before the apostles, and they prayed and laid their hands on them.

We see here that there are roles and responsibilities

that people are called to. As a new Christian I was not happy with authority and whilst I can see it now I could not see at the time that whilst I had zeal and enthusiasm I also lacked wisdom and I lacked maturity. Before I upset anyone, let me explain.

My attitude was in its bluntest form "Sorry I took so long to get here God but I am here now, so how about you and me get going on sorting this mess out" – I was referring to the church which clearly had been lacking one thing – Me!!!!!!!!! Only I could see what was wrong with it and God had been unable to do anything about it because he had been waiting for me to arrive.

That may sound more than a little ridiculous but as I say it is in its bluntest form exactly where I was at and is something I often see in others. Make no mistake there is no such thing as the perfect church but we do need to submit to Godly authority. It means becoming humble and letting go of our pride.

I have seen churches where highly successful entrepreneurs and business owners who are busy managing large work forces and handling million pound deals and contracts come to church and are accountable to labourers, retail assistants and farmhands.

It may mean losing our pride and admitting to our own faults, frustrations and hurts. We may need to accept that even though we now have the presence of Christ in our lives we may not actually be perfect and correct all the time, it will also allow us to grow and learn.

A word of caution is required though. We are not perfect and neither is anyone else. As I said churches are not buildings – they are people and the sole reason Christ came to earth is because people are incapable of being perfect.

Therefore we need to be aware that there are honourable people, struggling people and also players, actors, egotists and frauds in the church. With this in mind we need to know who it is safe to be open with. This is again why it is important to come under the authority of another.

If you have found the right church it will have a structure of accountability. This should be robust and allow you to know who is accountable to whom for their actions and who has the correct level of maturity to ensure you are being led by the good shepherds.

Ephesians 4:11-16 English Standard Version (ESV)

[11] And he gave the apostles, the prophets, the evangelists, the shepherds[a] and teachers,[b] [12] to equip the saints for the work of

ministry, for building up the body of Christ, ^{13} until we all attain to the unity of the faith and of the knowledge of the Son of God, to mature manhood,[c] to the measure of the stature of the fullness of Christ, ^{14} so that we may no longer be children, tossed to and fro by the waves and carried about by every wind of doctrine, by human cunning, by craftiness in deceitful schemes.

^{15} Rather, speaking the truth in love, we are to grow up in every way into him who is the head, into Christ,^{16} from whom the whole body, joined and held together by every joint with which it is equipped, when each part is working properly, makes the body grow so that it builds itself up in love.

1 Corinthians 12:28 English Standard Version (ESV)

^{28} And God has appointed in the church first apostles, second prophets, third teachers, then miracles, then gifts of healing, helping, administrating, and various kinds of tongues.

2 Timothy 1:11 English Standard Version (ESV)

^{11} for which I was appointed a preacher and apostle and teacher,

What we see here is that people are appointed to positions through Christ so that they can teach and disciple others. It is through this that our faith's able to grow and mature but we are not to remain solely as students.

Hebrews 5:12-14 English Standard Version (ESV)

12 For though by this time you ought to be teachers, you need someone to teach you again the basic principles of the oracles of God. You need milk, not solid food, 13 for everyone who lives on milk is unskilled in the word of righteousness, since he is a child. 14 But solid food is for the mature, for those who have their powers of discernment trained by constant practice to distinguish good from evil.

Our aim is to be in a place where we can eventually become teachers of those who come after us. Church is not to be simply an organised thing that is the responsibility of others to do for us.

We should be meeting and eating together, sharing and looking after one another. This does not require someone to always be organising although there may be some programmes within a church for this to ensure as in Acts chapter 6 no one is overlooked or taken advantage of.

Church is part of our everyday existence. We are church 24/7 and not just when we walk into a particular building.

We need to pray regularly

To be a Christian and not to pray is be human and never eat. Of all the constituents of the Christian life prayer has been the one that has been most corrupted by modern and old teaching alike. Some have made it deliberately complicated by adding conditions that are unbiblical or off-putting and others have made it remarkably simplistic and turned God in to some cosmic vending machine whereby you put in a prayer and pull out a blessing.

So let's firstly look at what prayer is and then we will look at how we do it.

Prayer is in its most straight forward description is simply talking WITH God. It is not however only talking TO God and asking for stuff.

The disciples in Matthew 6 ask Jesus to teach them pray and he shows them a pattern in what we now call the Lord's prayer, Later we see him praying himself in:

Matthew 11:25-26 English Standard Version Anglicised (ESVUK)

Come to Me, and I Will Give You Rest
25 At that time Jesus declared, "I thank you, Father, Lord of heaven and earth, that you have hidden these things from the wise and understanding and revealed them to little

children; ²⁶ yes, Father, for such was your gracious will.[a]

John 11:41-42 English Standard Version (ESV)

41 So they took away the stone. And Jesus lifted up his eyes and said, "Father, I thank you that you have heard me. 42 I knew that you always hear me, but I said this on account of the people standing around, that they may believe that you sent me."

John 12:28 English Standard Version (ESV)

²⁸ Father, glorify your name." Then a voice came from heaven: "I have glorified it, and I will glorify it again."

John 17 English Standard Version (ESV)

The High Priestly Prayer
17 When Jesus had spoken these words, he lifted up his eyes to heaven, and said, "Father, the hour has come; glorify your Son that the Son may glorify you, ² since you have given him authority over all flesh, to give eternal life to all whom you have given him. ³ And this is eternal life, that they know you, the only true God, and Jesus Christ whom you have sent. ⁴ I glorified you on earth, having accomplished the work that you gave me to do. ⁵ And now, Father, glorify me in your own presence with the glory that I had with you before the world existed.

⁶ *"I have manifested your name to the people whom you gave me out of the world. Yours they were, and you gave them to me, and they have kept your word. ⁷ Now they know that everything that you have given me is from you. ⁸ For I have given them the words that you gave me, and they have received them and have come to know in truth that I came from you; and they have believed that you sent me. ⁹ I am praying for them. I am not praying for the world but for those whom you have given me, for they are yours.*

¹⁰ *All mine are yours, and yours are mine, and I am glorified in them. ¹¹ And I am no longer in the world, but they are in the world, and I am coming to you. Holy Father, keep them in your name, which you have given me, that they may be one, even as we are one. ¹² While I was with them, I kept them in your name, which you have given me. I have guarded them, and not one of them has been lost except the son of destruction, that the Scripture might be fulfilled. ¹³ But now I am coming to you, and these things I speak in the world, that they may have my joy fulfilled in themselves.*

¹⁴ *I have given them your word, and the world has hated them because they are not of the world, just as I am not of the world. ¹⁵ I do not ask that you take them out of the world, but that you keep them from the evil one.[a] ¹⁶ They are not of the world, just as I am not of the world. ¹⁷ Sanctify*

them[b] in the truth; your word is truth. [18] As you sent me into the world, so I have sent them into the world. [19] And for their sake I consecrate myself,[c] that they also may be sanctified[d] in truth.
[20] "I do not ask for these only, but also for those who will believe in me through their word, [21] that they may all be one, just as you, Father, are in me, and I in you, that they also may be in us, so that the world may believe that you have sent me. [22] The glory that you have given me I have given to them, that they may be one even as we are one, [23] I in them and you in me, that they may become perfectly one, so that the world may know that you sent me and loved them even as you loved me.

[24] Father, I desire that they also, whom you have given me, may be with me where I am, to see my glory that you have given me because you loved me before the foundation of the world. [25] O righteous Father, even though the world does not know you, I know you, and these know that you have sent me. [26] I made known to them your name, and I will continue to make it known, that the love with which you have loved me may be in them, and I in them

He also prays three <u>prayers in the Garden of Gethsemane.</u>

Matthew 26:36-46 English Standard Version (ESV)

IS THAT IT?

Jesus Prays in Gethsemane
[36] Then Jesus went with them to a place called Gethsemane, and he said to his disciples, "Sit here, while I go over there and pray." [37] And taking with him Peter and the two sons of Zebedee, he began to be sorrowful and troubled. [38] Then he said to them, "My soul is very sorrowful, even to death; remain here, and watch[a] with me."

[39] And going a little farther he fell on his face and prayed, saying, "My Father, if it be possible, let this cup pass from me; nevertheless, not as I will, but as you will." [40] And he came to the disciples and found them sleeping. And he said to Peter, "So, could you not watch with me one hour? [41] Watch and pray that you may not enter into temptation. The spirit indeed is willing, but the flesh is weak." [42] Again, for the second time, he went away and prayed, "My Father, if this cannot pass unless I drink it, your will be done."

[43] And again he came and found them sleeping, for their eyes were heavy. [44] So, leaving them again, he went away and prayed for the third time, saying the same words again. [45] Then he came to the disciples and said to them, "Sleep and take your rest later on.[b] See, the hour is at hand, and the Son of Man is betrayed into the hands of sinners. [46] Rise, let us be going; see, my betrayer is at hand."

He prays on the cross - *"Father forgive them; for*

they know not what they do" (Luke 23:34) -"My God, My God, why hast thou forsaken me?" (Matt 27:46, Mark 15:34) - "Father, into thy hands I commit my spirit" (Luke 23:46)

Jesus does not change his way of speaking and he communicates praise, requests for others and requests for self.

We have over-complicated the whole idea of prayer and we need to strip it back to what it really is –

Prayer is communication WITH and not TO God.

Prayer is open, honest and real communication with God.

We do make our requests known to God as instructed in Philippians 4:6-7 and this is part of our prayer life. Our prayers though as all our conversations be they with God or each other should be shaped by our changing nature. As we become more Christ like and grow closer to him so to should the depth of our prayers.

Consider the growth of a child. At first that child only knows how to initiate conversation of sorts to reflect its own desires and wants. As it grows and matures it learns the joy of interaction and becomes aware of the needs of those around it. So to should our relationship with Christ grow and the nature of our prayers mature.

We will discover new means of communicating and also reasons other than to ask for ourselves. We will want to pray to say thank you and to give compliments (praise and worship), we will bring our concerns and cares for other to God not because we want to gossip but because we genuinely care about others and our requests may well be for our own desires but those will change as we develop a different set of priorities.

> We will
> Thank Jesus
> Ask for others and finally we will
> Pray for Yourself
> Do you see that? Jesus, others, then yourself.

We will pray in any combination of the four methods below:

- Pray out loud
- Pray silently
- Pray in private
- Pray with others

Just a quick note on this though – when we pray out loud with a others there must be a time of silence to hear as a group what Christ is saying to us. Which brings us nicely to another question.

Yeah, yeah I get all that talking simply and honestly to God stuff but what's all this a

listening stuff about – it freaks me out?

To be honest there are times when it freaks me out as well. It's a strange thing but in my early Christian life I prayed a lot and I saw my prayer requests coming to fruition. I had no doubt that God heard my prayers and got me out of more than a few sticky situations that my own stupidity had got me into.

(That is not to say that he lets me get away with anything I shouldn't though).

Therefore I know I am praying to God and that he is there. I could even accept that sometimes there were circumstances and situations that arose and people would ask me "so what do you think God is saying to you through that?" My problem was that there were people who told me God spoke to them directly and God told them to do things.

I had seen the films, read the books and watched the documentaries and to my mind this was the sort of thing serial killers and people with severe mental health problems said to explain why they killed or covered their walls with tin foil. It has become a little bit of a cliché but yes my view was that when I spoke to God I prayed but when God spoke to others they were mad.

As a new Christian I would diligently make time to

pray every day. It was a pretty standard prayer which I would pray at the start of the day before going of to work or at night before saying Amen and going to sleep. If a situation changed then it was an answer to prayer and if it didn't then it meant God was not particularly bothered or did not care.

As I learnt to sit still and wait I found that something strange happened. It was not that some audible voice told me a solution but that I began to find solutions and courses of action coming into my thoughts. In the interests of openness and honesty I must admit that my initial feeling was that as I was taking time to think about things I was coming up with these solutions in my own strength.

However I then had several events when I realised that I was being prompted to do or say things that were not rational or within my nature. When we pray about a situation and expect God to act it may be that if we shut up and listen he will tell us what we need to do to change the situation.

The expectation in the prayers without listening is that we expect God to make everything alright when he is saying that if we listen he will tell us what to do to change it and from that we learn to live in a more Christ like manner.

Understanding what it means to say Christ is

speaking to us is essential. It is not always an audible voice as some super-spiritual people may have us believe. It is not an auditory hallucination either.

There are many ways God speaks to us. Consider the Christmas story. God spoke to Mary through an angel, Joseph through a dream, the shepherds through a group of angels and the wise men through a star. He spoke to each of them in a way they understood and in a language they understood.

The Bible tells us a number of ways God speaks

- In person (Adam and Eve)
- Through a burning bush (Moses)
- An audible voice(Moses and John the Baptist)
- Through nature (David)
- Through other people (David and Israel, Jonah and Nineveh)
- Through Angels (appearing as strangers)
- Through animals (Bàlaam)
- The stars and clouds (wise men and the Israelites in the wilderness)
- Through restlessness and conscience (Darius and Jacob)
- Dreams (Joseph (both Jesus father and the old testament prophet as well as Daniel and Jacob).

These days there are even more ways he speaks to people including the Bible and the Holy Spirit.

I know of times when a recurring song or a few lines from a song do not leave my thoughts until I have taken time to consider them and relate them to something going on in my life.

I can also tell stories of other people who have been sure that something occurring during a drug related experience was the only way God could get through to them or the person who found every time he switched his television on it seemed to be selecting a different channel to the one it had been last on and the subject matter of the programme was the same each time as if someone was telling him something,

I have had a similar experience to this with my radio. Others tell of how they kept coming across the same type of problem wherever they went until they dealt with something within them self. They then found that they never came across that situation again. I met someone else who saw things happening repeatedly to people all around them in a short space of time. When they eventually spoke to someone to voice their feeling that God was trying to tell them something, they did something about it.

God speaks to us in ways we will listen and we can pray in ways that are real to us. Three people can sit on a mountain top. The first can pick up a bible to read out loud or recite scripture from memory and then lay back and allow its meaning to penetrate their being and thoughts. Another recalls or sings a song. Its goes round and round and its meaning and sentiments resonate a word about the majesty of Christ.

The third person appears to be staring out into the atmosphere but in fact something has caught their eye and they are contemplating the power of this person who so perfectly created the place where they are and how anything we may create simply cannot improve or even match the beauty of what he has done.

As they descend the mountain every one of them has received the same word/message but each of them has received it in their own way. This is not the God to whom we pray but with whom we pray.

We need to tell others about our choice

So often things work on a spiritual and human level. When we share our faith, four important factors come into play –

- We publicly assert our beliefs which reinforces them to ourselves and forces us to defend them and to receive encouragement
- We make ourselves open to be challenged and through that to grow

- We open doors to say more
- We obey Christ

By making that public statement of our beliefs we commit ourselves to what we have decided to do. Believers and sceptics alike will challenge us. The sceptics will try and dispute the truth of what we believe or if we are true to what we say and the believers will be an encouragement.

Both will lead us back to the bible and encourage us to check our understanding of what it says or whether what we are being told is truth. This brings us to the next step which is to become part of a group that studies the bible together.

Become part of a regular bible study group

We need to study scripture together and not alone. Once again taking a personal example, At one time I would only read the bible alone because then I could pretend it always asserted that I was right. I could read anything I wanted in the bible and see how it showed me that I was right and even if the rest of the world disagreed at least me and God were right.

Being part of a bible study group was an eye opener because then I had to be challenged to look at the bigger picture and to actually look at the bits of the bible that I would have preferred to continue pretending did not exist.

Recently with the use of increased access to media there has become a glut of false teaching masquerading as Christian teaching. I have tried in the past to type various preposterous ideas into internet search engines and have never found one that has not already been thought of and justified by some teacher or other.

To be fair I am not talking about silliness such as Jesus rode into Jerusalem on a unicorn but that is not as far removed from some of the stuff you can find as some might think. We need to meet with other Christians in a place where we can learn from the wisdom of the mature and be inspired by the energy of the young. I am talking about spiritually not necessarily physically old and young.

Father, Spirit, Son – What's That All About?

The Trinity is something that may or may not have been an issue to you prior to becoming a Christian but it will not be long before people start asking you about it and finding out your views on the Trinity.

Understanding the Trinity is a difficulty for many people and is one of those areas that has caused more arguments and difficulties than is healthy. It is quite right that we understand who God is and that is high on the list of things we should be sure about if we are going to discern false teaching but sadly the Trinity has been hijacked by the judgemental and hyper critical to use as a tool to batter anyone and everyone they want to prove themselves to be better than.

Sadly people have been criticised and discredited simply based on an out of place word or misunderstood term. Because of this, I was tempted not to include a section on the Trinity in this series for fear of not having enough knowledge or in case I used a wrong term that could somehow lead to the whole series being considered false. However as I read up on some stuff I realised the reasoning behind much of this misunderstanding.

Let us start with some basic truths.

There is only one God. (1 Corinthians 8:4; Galatians 3:20; 1 Timothy 2:5).

God has three parts Father, Son, and Spirit. (Matthew 3:16-17, Matthew 28:19 28:19; 2 Corinthians 13:14).

These three parts all have separate and distinct personalities. (Hebrews 1:8-9, John 6:27; Romans 1:7; 1 Peter 1:2, John 1:1, 14; Romans 9:5; Colossians 2:9; Hebrews 1:8; 1 John 5:20 Acts 5:3-4; 1 Corinthians 3:16).

Now hopefully none of that has offended anyone yet although perhaps the term separate will give some people scope to pick holes. Over the years there have been various ways in which the Trinity has been popularly explained and various criticisms made of all these explanations. Here are a few –

The three leaves on clover – they are all part of the clover but have their own identities – however this has been criticised because the leaves all play the same role and are attached to a stem which is also part of the clover.

The egg. It has three parts – the shell, the white and

the yolk. This has been criticised as the egg is only the sum part of these but no one part can be called an egg on its own.

H2O is all made up the same but exists in three different forms, liquid (water), gas (steam) or solid (ice). This has been criticised but the parts are so interchangeable and any part can become another

The human being has three parts mind, body and spirit and all these parts are the essence of the person but they are created.

The difficulty with all of these though is that we are trying to describe the creator through the created which is a little bit like trying to use a Tornado Fighter Plane to describe the Wright Brothers or even a Mondeo Estate to describe Henry Ford. God is bigger than anything he has created and that includes the human mind.

When we as Christians refer to God we are referring to God the Father, God the Son and God the Holy Spirit. When we refer to Our Father in Heaven, Jesus Christ or the Holy Spirit we are naming a single part of God and yet at the same time (at the risk of being accused of heresy) we are also referring to God as a whole.

In reading up on this part of the study it became clear to me as to why it is so wrong to try and be

P.C and suggest that Jews, Christians and Muslim all worship the same God. For some time as I looked at the root of the three major faiths I fell into this trap of believing that we all began harmoniously worshipping the same God then Abraham did the wrong thing with Hagar and because of this Hagar and Ishmael were banished and their descendants continued to worship the same God.

However, God fell out with the descendants of Isaac, then in the next chapter Jesus Christ comes to earth to put a lot of stuff right. But some of the descendants of Abraham do not believe he is who he says he is and reject him but those who believe in him continue to worship the same God as Isaacs descendants and Ishmaels do but also recognise Jesus as his son.

Unfortunately this is not true because Jesus is not only the Son of God but also God. Therefore to say we all worship the same God is not true because our God is made up of three parts and includes the person of Jesus Christ which in fact make him very different to God without Christ.

The Trinity is a Christian truth. Please do not allow terminology and words to cause division and friction.

Spirit or Ghost

One thing that I have heard some people get really uppity about is whether they should refer to the Holy Spirit or the Holy Ghost. This though is a matter of understanding the origins and evolution of language. Ghost was the spiritual being of a person not the modern version of the word.

Therefore when someone refers to the Holy Ghost or the Holy Spirit they are referring to the same person. Personally because of the way the use of the word ghost has evolved I prefer to use the word spirit because ghost suggests the essence of a dead being rather than living one.

Forgiveness – Can I Keep On Sinning Then?

I'm Accepted, I'm forgiven – can I do it all again?

When Jesus was crucified as the perfect sacrifice for our sin, he took on the price of all sin past, present and future. That is the good news for us all. However there are riders to this that are often overlooked. In our haste to share the good news we can omit certain factors.

1. All who repent and call on the name of the Lord will be forgiven (Romans 10;13)
2. If we forgive others then we will be forgiven but if we REFUSE to forgive then God will not forgive us (Matthew 6;15)
3. We are instructed by Christ to pray that we will be forgiven in the same measure as we forgive others (Matthew 6:12)
4. Paul tells us in 2 Corinthians 5:17 that we who are Christians are new creations and are no longer the same people we were before this goes also for how we see others.

Receiving Christ's forgiveness and giving forgiveness ourselves are closely connected.

Christ's forgiveness does indeed mean all our sins are washed away. However this does not mean we can keep on sinning because we will always be forgiven, that is craziness talking.

Romans 6:1-4 English Standard Version (ESV)

Dead to Sin, Alive to God
6 What shall we say then? Are we to continue in sin that grace may abound? ² By no means! How can we who died to sin still live in it? ³ Do you not know that all of us who have been baptized into Christ Jesus were baptized into his death? ⁴ We were buried therefore with him by baptism into death, in order that, just as Christ was raised from the dead by the glory of the Father, we too might walk in newness of life.

There is conscious sin that needs repentance, Be aware though that after salvation the pain of repentance always, always outweighs any pleasure or satisfaction derived from the sin. Unconscious sin (those sins we may commit unwittingly) will be brought to our attention by the conviction of the Holy Spirit.

The Holy Spirit will make us aware of the fact that this is wrong and then we can repent and move on. Finally there is what we may call a weakness or repeated sin. In Christian Jargon this is often referred to as a besetting sin.

We know these things are wrong and we struggle and fight against them. We actually hate these sins but we keep messing up. This is nothing new and anyone who claims to be free of such sin suggests themselves better than the apostle Paul.

Romans 7:15-20 English Standard Version (ESV)

[15] For I do not understand my own actions. For I do not do what I want, but I do the very thing I hate. [16] Now if I do what I do not want, I agree with the law, that it is good. [17] So now it is no longer I who do it, but sin that dwells within me. [18] For I know that nothing good dwells in me, that is, in my flesh. For I have the desire to do what is right, but not the ability to carry it out. [19] For I do not do the good I want, but the evil I do not want is what I keep on doing. [20] Now if I do what I do not want, it is no longer I who do it, but sin that dwells within me.

Please be aware that we cannot con Christ. We cannot convince him that our conscious choice driven sin is a besetting sin that we are fighting against. Christ is in the process of transforming us and he will set us free but sometimes that is not immediate and it teaches us to lean on him and to learn to be compassionate to others.

As a child I was taught to say sorry and apologise when I did wrong. I recall being told of in school and sent back to a teacher I had been rude and disrespectful to. I was told to apologise. Given the choice between further punishment and saying sorry the choice was easy.

I went back to him and said sorry, the teacher seemed to relish the apology and demanded that I tell him what I was apologising for and tell him why it was wrong. This I did on the surface.

However with each sentence I was completing the ending in silence and all the time my mouth was saying sorry my heart was saying "you deserved it you **** and if you think that was bad, wait and see what else is coming your way". We cannot play this game with God. He knows our heart and it is no good praying a repentant prayer if we do not feel or mean it in our heart.

Forgiveness is a three way thing between God, us and others.

- If we want to be forgiven we need to repent genuinely and be willing to forgive others
- We must repeatedly forgive the repentant
- We must love those in unconscious sin or unaware of their sin
- We must continue to love the unrepentant to a point that they too will come to repentance.

Worship, Praise and Prayer

Christians are simply people who share one thing in common. Admittedly it is quite a large thing and it should shape their character and the way they behave. However they are individuals with different characters, personalities and interests. We all believe that Jesus Christ is both God and the Son, he came to earth in human form to pay the price for our sins and we have given our lives and bodies over to him to own and direct.

Other than that we are all very different. I drafted this whilst sitting in church waiting for the meeting to begin. I am surrounded by people most of whom I would probably never have met or crossed paths with outside of this setting. It is not that I imagine myself any better than others here or less than them just that we are all from different backgrounds, ages and interest groups.

We are all different and we all have different ways of expressing ourselves. In a moment the music will start and we will start singing or rather some of us will and then there will come a time of open prayer.

When the music starts some people will jump up

excitedly. They will clap and stick their hands in the air, they will clap and make some happy sounds in addition to the words on the screen. At the same time as they are doing this there will be others who remain seated, they may well drop the heads, close their eyes and the words they sing may barely be audible.

The majority will fill a space somewhere in-between these extremes. When the music fades and the singing stops there will be a time of open prayer. Some will remain standing or stand up. They will shout their prayers very loudly (presumably to get Gods attention). They may wave their arms around a bit and display a variety of emotions.

Others may appear to deliver a monotone monologue. Their words will be sincere but their emotions/feelings remain guarded to mortal ears. Others remain seated. Heads bowed, eyes shut and hands together as per tradition. They remain silent bringing their prayers of agreement and requests to God in silence and listening. Some may question why they are there in a prayer meeting when they remain silent but when we pray God hears the silent prayers as clearly as he hears the loud and emotional ones.

So why do I write all this. It is just to explain that

when it comes to Praise and Worship and Prayer we all do it in our own way according to how Christ has made us. As long as the act is an honest act between our self and God, there is no right and wrong simply different ways of doing the same thing.

It is a sad fact that the subject of worship and style of worship has become such a defining feature of many churches. Worship has become the means by which many people judge the quality and truth of the teaching and the people there.

If you were to ask the majority of Christians to describe the church they attend they will begin by describing it as lively, traditional or some other way of describing the way they "do" the worship bit and by that they mean the singing.

Depending on the preconceived ideas of the person we may draw our own conclusions about the churches spiritual condition by how the worship is described.

A hands in the air lively church will be seen by some as either Holy Spirit led with an awareness of the gifts of the spirit or by others as having superficial and shallow teaching aimed at attracting young at heart people with little interest in the mature person looking for a depth of faith.

IS THAT IT?

A church with a more traditional style of worship with maybe an old style organ and old hymns is considered dry and boring in its teaching appealing to head knowledge and not the Spirit whilst others may see a deep and reverent atmosphere that shows due respect and awe to the majesty of Christ.

The truth is that worship is not just about the songs and/or hymns we sing. It is about the heart and spirit behind the way we sing them, the way we pray, how we read and study scripture, the way we live and the way we speak of Christ/God/the Spirit.

However for the moment we are talking about the music and song styles. During a recent conversation a friend of mine described a popular modern hymn/chorus as the Christian version of "Wonderwall".

His words resonated strongly with me as I have been in services and celebrations where that particular song could just as easily been replaced with Wonderwall and the singers would probably have sung it with just as much passion and atmosphere. It is not that the tune or the words defined the quality of the worship or the nature of the church. It is the heart of the people and the teaching.

I enjoy real, genuine praise and worship music however it is very rare that you will find me standing in church with my hands in the air jumping up and down yelling the words to any hymn or song at 80 decibels. This not because I believe it to be wrong to be so demonstrative in worship but that my singing voice really should have been banned under the Geneva Convention.

I have watched as people visibly move away as I start trying to sing. I do however have an extensive and eclectic mix of praise and worship music and I do enjoy being a part of that bit of the service however it is done as long as it is genuine and passionate. It makes no odds to me if we are singing a 400 year old hymn, a 1970s Country and Western Classic, a screaming guitar hard rock sound, a modern song or a cheesy 1980s song.

If the heart is there then its real and you can sense the presence of Christ and his spirit in the place. My particular taste in music would be the rock sound but I have thrown away CD's and deleted music from my collection from the rock genre simply because the artist appears to have forgotten who they are singing to or about, (or possibly thought that Christians will buy any old tat).

There are artists and churches where the songs can be sung and "performed" note perfect and the "audience" sing along smiling and happy but again the room is devoid of anything remotely spiritual.

When we consider where we want to worship we need to base our decision on the place Christ wants us to be. We should consider the accountability and the truth of what is being taught before the style of worship. Yes it matters but if the choice is between a place lacking somewhat in the area of worship or lacking in its teaching or accountability then we know what our choice should be.

What's All This Tongues Business About?

As a child I was forced to attend church. I would be dragged from one church to another every Sunday. They were very staid Methodist churches where we would stand and sing a hymn, sit down and hear a bible reading (or if we were lucky as children a special talk).

Then we would listen to the notices and have the collection before we had another sing-song followed by the long, long prayer that was said by the preacher/minister who would then end it with a cue for us all to join together in the prayer Jesus taught us.

Then we could sing another hymn and listen to another reading before another hymn and then a long, long talk that in fact should not exceed twenty minutes and a final hymn.

So then imagine my surprise when I went to a slightly less choreographed church service but the bit that blew me apart was the part when people started making bizarre noises and sounds that I was informed were talking in tongues.

Over the course of my early Christian life tongues caused me a lot of confusion and I witnessed a lot of division as a result of it. Initially people I knew well told me that speaking in tongues was the realm of the strange people and questionable Christians. I was told to stay well away from any church that engaged in such activity.

To be fair this was something I was more than happy to agree with because it was freaky and scary stuff. However I had a struggle because there were people I knew through people I knew who were part of these churches and apart from this odd behaviour in church they seemed perfectly decent and rational people who were not prone to strange behaviour or weirdness.

So despite my fears and scepticism I did cautiously dip into these places from time to time but then I had another issue. If at one extreme there were those who claimed people speaking in tongues were exhibitionists wanting to draw attention to themselves through some outdated and/or misunderstood bible reading then at the other end of the scale there were those who were telling me that I HAD to talk in tongues.

Otherwise I was not truly a Christian and was therefore unsaved and hurtling towards hell in a handcart. All this did for me was confuse me and I questioned the validity of everything else that either side were saying.

So let's take a look at what the bible says on the subject:

Matthew 7:16 English Standard Version (ESV)

¹⁶ You will recognize them by their fruits. Are grapes gathered from thornbushes, or figs from thistles?

Mark 16:17 English Standard Version (ESV)

¹⁷ And these signs will accompany those who believe: in my name they will cast out demons; they will speak in new tongues;

Acts 2:1-12 English Standard Version (ESV)

The Coming of the Holy Spirit
2 When the day of Pentecost arrived, they were all together in one place. ² And suddenly there came from heaven a sound like a mighty rushing wind, and it filled the entire house where they were sitting. ³ And divided tongues as of fire appeared to them and rested[a] on each one of them. ⁴ And they were all filled with the Holy Spirit and began to speak in other tongues as the Spirit gave them utterance.
⁵ Now there were dwelling in Jerusalem Jews, devout men from every nation under heaven. ⁶ And at this sound the multitude came

together, and they were bewildered, because each one was hearing them speak in his own language. ⁷ And they were amazed and astonished, saying, "Are not all these who are speaking Galileans? ⁸ And how is it that we hear, each of us in his own native language? ⁹ Parthians and Medes and Elamites and residents of Mesopotamia, Judea and Cappadocia, Pontus and Asia, ¹⁰ Phrygia and Pamphylia, Egypt and the parts of Libya belonging to Cyrene, and visitors from Rome, ¹¹ both Jews and proselytes, Cretans and Arabians—we hear them telling in our own tongues the mighty works of God." ¹² And all were amazed and perplexed, saying to one another, "What does this mean?"

Acts 19:5-7 English Standard Version (ESV)

⁵ On hearing this, they were baptized in[a] the name of the Lord Jesus. ⁶ And when Paul had laid his hands on them, the Holy Spirit came on them, and they began speaking in tongues and prophesying. ⁷ There were about twelve men in all.

1 Corinthians 12:4-10 English Standard Version (ESV)

⁴ Now there are varieties of gifts, but the same Spirit; ⁵ and there are varieties of service, but the same Lord; ⁶ and there are varieties of activities, but it is the same God who empowers them all in everyone. ⁷ To each is given the manifestation of the Spirit for the common good.[8] For to one is given through the Spirit the utterance of wisdom, and to another the utterance of knowledge according to the same Spirit, [9] to another faith by the same Spirit, to another gifts of healing by the one Spirit, [10] to another the working of miracles, to another prophecy, to another the ability to distinguish between spirits, to another various kinds of tongues, to another the interpretation of tongues.

<u>1 Corinthians 12:28-30 English Standard Version (ESV)</u>

[28] And God has appointed in the church first apostles, second prophets, third teachers, then miracles, then gifts of healing, helping, administrating, and various kinds of tongues. [29] Are all apostles? Are all prophets? Are all teachers? Do all work miracles? [30] Do all possess gifts of healing? Do all speak with tongues? Do all interpret?

<u>1 Corinthians 13:1-2 English Standard Version (ESV)</u>

The Way of Love
13 If I speak in the tongues of men and of angels, but have not love, I am a noisy gong or a clanging cymbal. [2] And if I have prophetic powers, and understand all mysteries and all knowledge, and if I have all faith, so as to remove mountains, but

have not love, I am nothing.

1 Corinthians 14:1-30 English Standard Version (ESV)

Prophecy and Tongues
14 Pursue love, and earnestly desire the spiritual gifts, especially that you may prophesy. ² For one who speaks in a tongue speaks not to men but to God; for no one understands him, but he utters mysteries in the Spirit. ³ On the other hand, the one who prophesies speaks to people for their upbuilding and encouragement and consolation. ⁴ The one who speaks in a tongue builds up himself, but the one who prophesies builds up the church. ⁵ Now I want you all to speak in tongues, but even more to prophesy. The one who prophesies is greater than the one who speaks in tongues, unless someone interprets, so that the church may be built up.
⁶ Now, brothers,[a] if I come to you speaking in tongues, how will I benefit you unless I bring you some revelation or knowledge or prophecy or teaching? ⁷ If even lifeless instruments, such as the flute or the harp, do not give distinct notes, how will anyone know what is played? ⁸ And if the bugle gives an indistinct sound, who will get ready for battle? ⁹ So with yourselves, if with your tongue you utter speech that is not intelligible, how will anyone know what is said? For you will be speaking into the air. ¹⁰ There are doubtless many different languages in the world, and none is without meaning, ¹¹ but if I do not know the

meaning of the language, I will be a foreigner to the speaker and the speaker a foreigner to me. [12] So with yourselves, since you are eager for manifestations of the Spirit, strive to excel in building up the church.

[13] Therefore, one who speaks in a tongue should pray that he may interpret. [14] For if I pray in a tongue, my spirit prays but my mind is unfruitful. [15] What am I to do? I will pray with my spirit, but I will pray with my mind also; I will sing praise with my spirit, but I will sing with my mind also. [16] Otherwise, if you give thanks with your spirit, how can anyone in the position of an outsider[b] say "Amen" to your thanksgiving when he does not know what you are saying? [17] For you may be giving thanks well enough, but the other person is not being built up. [18] I thank God that I speak in tongues more than all of you. [19] Nevertheless, in church I would rather speak five words with my mind in order to instruct others, than ten thousand words in a tongue.

[20] Brothers, do not be children in your thinking. Be infants in evil, but in your thinking be mature. [21] In the Law it is written, "By people of strange tongues and by the lips of foreigners will I speak to this people, and even then they will not listen to me, says the Lord." [22] Thus tongues are a sign not for believers but for unbelievers, while prophecy is a sign[c] not for unbelievers but for believers. [23] If, therefore, the whole church comes together and all speak in tongues, and outsiders or

unbelievers enter, will they not say that you are out of your minds?[24] *But if all prophesy, and an unbeliever or outsider enters, he is convicted by all, he is called to account by all,* [25] *the secrets of his heart are disclosed, and so, falling on his face, he will worship God and declare that God is really among you.*

Orderly Worship
[26] *What then, brothers? When you come together, each one has a hymn, a lesson, a revelation, a tongue, or an interpretation. Let all things be done for building up.* [27] *If any speak in a tongue, let there be only two or at most three, and each in turn, and let someone interpret.* [28] *But if there is no one to interpret, let each of them keep silent in church and speak to himself and to God.* [29] *Let two or three prophets speak, and let the others weigh what is said.* [30] *If a revelation is made to another sitting there, let the first be silent.*

Galatians 5:19-24 English Standard Version (ESV)

[19] *Now the works of the flesh are evident: sexual immorality, impurity, sensuality,* [20] *idolatry, sorcery, enmity, strife, jealousy, fits of anger, rivalries, dissensions, divisions,* [21] *envy, [a] drunkenness, orgies, and things like these. I warn you, as I warned you before, that those who do[b] such things will not inherit the kingdom of God.* [22] *But the fruit of the Spirit is love, joy, peace, patience, kindness, goodness, faithfulness,*

²³ gentleness, self-control; against such things there is no law. ²⁴ And those who belong to Christ Jesus have crucified the flesh with its passions and desires.

I have deliberately included a massive amount of scripture here to ensure we do not omit anything. Clearly when we look at this subject it has long been a subject of discussion and debate.

Now we could share our personal views on the subject of speaking in tongues and praying in tongues (is there a difference?) but will leave it to you to look at the readings and discuss with your trusted advisors.

Denominations and "*Demon*inations"

Much has been made of the fact that there are many types of Christian church and a variety of interpretations of what it means to be a Christian. This has resulted in a great misunderstanding of what Christianity is. Sadly we as Christians can add to the confusion by identifying ourselves as Anglicans, Baptists, Methodists, Free Church, Presbyterians, Pentecostal or any number of other label. We may then get embroiled in disputes as to why we are right and someone else down the road is wrong.

In truth the vast majority of these labels or to give them their correct name denominations agree on the very basics of the faith and amongst the rational people there is no tension. Broadly (and it is very broadly) speaking what the denominations boil down to is styles, governing bodies, priorities and emphasis. For example some prefer to have loud praise music that raises the roof whilst others have more contemplative music. Some place an emphasis on social mission work, others place a lot of emphasis on the works of the Holy Spirit and the power he channels through us and others concentrate on developing a personal relationship with Christ. Some churches prefer the consistency of having the same person sharing the messages and leading the worship every week whilst others believe it is better to have a variety of people with different styles and emphasis bringing the message.

Within many denominations there will be a variety of churches that work in their own (God led) way. For example in many a town (and even some villages) you may visit two or more Baptist or Methodist Churches and they may be very different experiences. Any suggestion that one church has everything correct and proper whilst all others are at fault and completely wrong would be a warning sign that the fault lies with the one that claims to have it all sorted out.

Another common misconception is that you cannot go to any church other than your own one. This is not true. If we are Christians we are part of one body therefore we are all part of one church. As such we are free to visit other churches and to mix with one another. However we should all have a home church where we come under the authority of one person or body and we are accountable to one another and we have responsibility for others.

We should also be cautious to confess ourselves as

Christians or Believers rather than by a denomination. I am not a Methodist neither am I free Church or a Presbyterian. I am a Christian. I am a follower of Jesus Christ not of a particular Confession, Statement of Belief or Creed. That is not to say that I do not believe the statements of belief to be factual merely that if it is true then it is true because it came first from Jesus Christ.

For information only here is a quick and extremely basic history guide to the denominations of church you may find. A knowledge of church history however basic and extensive will not serve to enhance our salvation or make us a better or superior example of Christ like living.

What it will do though is help us to understand what some people are talking about when they talk of the church they are a part of or when people advise us to stay away from one church or go to another or convince us that they go to the only church in the entire world that is right. It will hopefully help us to avoid falling into the trap of being high and mighty about our understanding of Christ and cynical of anyone who does not attend the same church that we do.

It will help us understand and accept that our brothers and sisters in Christ are not better or worse than us simply because they "do" church differently to us. In addition to this please be clear that there are good people who walk close with Christ and are saved who are attending compromised churches that are not teaching the full gospel or are teaching falsehoods. There are churches that may be teaching truth whilst organizationally they sign up to compromise, (this is a recurring theme in church history).

Jesus appeared to the disciples and others on a number of occasions after the resurrection and instructed them (Matthew 28) to take the gospel to the world. They did this and they did it very successfully at the cost to their lives and liberty. Most notably they reached Asia Minor, the Middle East and Europe (Italy, Turkey, and Greece).

Thomas in particular is worthy of note as he spread the gospel message to India. They did not have the bible as we have it today but they did have the Torah (the first five books) and most of the Old Testament books. However the news of Jesus Christ was from their first hand testimonies of what they had seen and heard from him.

Churches met in people's homes and they shared all things and listened to the apostles teachings either directly or through letters read aloud to them from the apostles. They were persecuted as Christ was and Stephen who was not one of the twelve apostles was the first martyr to be killed for sharing the gospel. Paul (previously called Saul) came to faith. He never met Christ when he walked the earth in human form and he became a prolific evangelist and wrote most of the letters that make up the books of the New Testament. Alongside Paul were Barnabas, Timothy and Titus who became teachers in their own right. The church in Corinth needed to be challenged by Paul because they had begun to follow the teachers rather than Christ.

The Roman leaders were unable to deal with this new faith and in 313AD the Roman Leader Constantine decided the best way to control these new-fangled Christian types was to integrate their faith into the Roman religions and then enforce it as the faith of the Empire. In 380AD Theodius called this faith Catholicism.

The Romans created a Bishop of Rome (later referred to as the Pope) and venerated ancient relics as having power and Mary as the mediator between people and Christ with other "Holy" people. The Bishop of Rome is allegedly always a direct descendant of Peter because of the reading below.

Matthew 16:16-18 English Standard Version (ESV)

[16] Simon Peter replied, "You are the Christ, the

Son of the living God."[17] And Jesus answered him, "Blessed are you, Simon Bar-Jonah! For flesh and blood has not revealed this to you, but my Father who is in heaven. [18] And I tell you, you are Peter, and on this rock[a] I will build my church, and the gates of hell[b] shall not prevail against it.

Despite the attempts of the Roman leaders to control the Christians there remained an underground movement. This movement continued to stick rigidly to the teachings of Christ and this remained predominantly in the eastern reaches of the Empire.

The Bible, in its present form (66 books divided between the Old and New Testaments), appeared firstly in around 381AD. This was in Constantinople (previously Byzantium and currently Istanbul). The original text was in a variety of languages due to the fact that it was written by a variety of people. At around 400AD St Jerome translated the whole bible into Latin and that was the way it stayed until Wycliffe in the 1300s translated some of it into Common English and then Tyndale in the 1500s bit by bit and then the Authorised King James Bible in 1611.

In 1511 Martin Luther along with others challenged vociferously the teachings and structure of the dominant Catholic Church in Europe. Cutting a long story short, the Protest(ant) churches were created. They challenged the authority of Rome, financial bribes to gain access to heaven, purgatory and the need for a mediator between God and Humans.

In effect there now existed three types of Church. The dominant Catholic Church that ruled from Rome, The Orthodox churches that held to Christs teaching but mixed in some rituals from the synagogues of their roots in Judaism and the Protestant churches, which for the most part rejected the teachings of Rome about the Bishop of Rome, confessionals, the saints, and a number of other things.

The Protestants thought also for the most part continued with some of the stuff from Rome that suited the needs of those in power. So they refused to allow the bible to be translated into a common language on the basis that the peasants (who could read and write) were too stupid to be able to understand and interpret it (or those who could understand it may start a revolution).

The leaders of most protestant churches in Britain were the third sons of the ruling elite. The first son took the business the second led an army regiment and third became a member of the clergy. Two events in particular saw a massive change in Britain. Henry VIII married Catherine of Aragon (a

Catholic) but Henry began an affair with Anne Boleyn whose family were strong Protestants.

To get around this Henry simply decided to become a protestant and set up the Church of England. What we now had were two strong religious voices in Britain each serving its own needs rather than Christ, However Anne Boleyn despite her adulterous affair and marriage to Henry was a strong believer in the translation of the bible into common English and promoted this view.

It all gets a bit complicated now but the end result was that Henrys successor James 1st commissioned the King James Bible which drew much of its content from Tyndale's translation. People had continued throughout time to receive divine revelation from Christ but now they had the word of God written by him through the people to the people in their own language.

The Protestant church however was not perfect. People were free to express their views and their ways of worship but it was still controlled by the wealthy and used by them and the monarchy to control people.

Oliver Cromwell and notable Puritans such as John Bunyan and Thomas Watson challenged the Political and Spiritual beliefs of the church as well as the wealth and this began the growth of the free churches in that they were free from state control. Many others becoming literate and educated grew to challenge widely held views and question practices such as slavery etc. Many remained within the Anglican (Church of England) Church but were forced to leave.

The Wesley brothers created the Methodist Church not through choice but due to being ostracized. They developed a structure that was democratic, compassionate and took social responsibility seriously and as a priority.

The Baptists disagreed with the practice of infant baptism amongst other things. Many other denominations and independent churches grew from these three denominations. Most differ very little in their core beliefs but predominantly in their styles of worship, teaching, emphasis and/or structure.

It saddens me when I hear people say that a person is not a Christian because they belong to a particular type of church or they can't be a Christian if they think a certain way about a particular part of doctrine. In truth if you are to ask any person with a true and genuine relationship with Jesus Christ they will tell you that they have questions over their denominational statement of belief (if they are even aware of it) and even some of the teaching they hear in or from their church or its leaders. It is the sign of a seeking believer as opposed to the blind follower.

To accuse a person of not being a Christian because they disagree with our understanding is very judgemental and stinks of pride. It suggests the person believes they have the monopoly on being correct and only those who agree with them can be saved.

So how do we determine the differences between the true Church of Jesus Christ and cults/false teaching? It is quite simple really -

A true Church of Christ teaches –

1. Salvation by grace not works
2. Christ is the only way to salvation
3. We pray directly to God (Father/Son/Spirit)
4. The trinity of God in three persons
5. The gifts and fruits of the spirit

A true Church of Christ does not teach

1. Anything other than Heaven or Hell as our destination after physical death
2. A need for a mediator in prayers
3. Salvation through works and financial gifts
4. Health/Wealth/Comfort as a reward for faith and works
5. Heavy Shepherding (controlling behaviour

from leaders)

A true Church of Christ does not demand

1. Total submission to the leadership
2. A membership fee
3. Places of privilege
4. A dress code
5. Acts of service
6. Demand differs from advises

A true church of Christ has

1. Accountability process for the leaders
2. An openness to ask and learn
3. Room for growth

Additional to all this be very wary no matter how scripturally sound the teachings of any church where the leader is held in reverence above Christ. Do the people quote the speaker/leader or Jesus Christ?

I Thought Life Was Meant to Get Easier

One of the sad things about recent witnessing and evangelism (telling people about Jesus and why they need to come to know him) has been the move towards the life goes easier with a bit of Jesus and that if you behave yourself and do everything right then life is a beautiful ride in the comfort and wealth of the world.

I am not going to waste too much time on this garbage but instead will show you just a few New Testament readings and some stories from the more recent years.

Mark 13:9-13 English Standard Version (ESV)

⁹ "But be on your guard. For they will deliver you over to councils, and you will be beaten in synagogues, and you will stand before governors and kings for my sake, to bear witness before them. ¹⁰ And the gospel must first be proclaimed to all nations. ¹¹ And when they bring you to trial and deliver you over, do not be anxious beforehand what you are to say, but say whatever is given you in that hour, for it is not you who speak, but the Holy Spirit. ¹² And brother will deliver brother *over to death, and the father his child, and children will rise against parents and have them put to death. ^{13} And you will be hated by all for my name's sake. But the one who endures to the end will be saved.*

Acts 12:1-4 English Standard Version (ESV)

James Killed and Peter Imprisoned
12 About that time Herod the king laid violent hands on some who belonged to the church. 2 He killed James the brother of John with the sword, 3 and when he saw that it pleased the Jews, he proceeded to arrest Peter also. This was during the days of Unleavened Bread. 4 And when he had seized him, he put him in prison, delivering him over to four squads of soldiers to guard him, intending after the Passover to bring him out to the people.

2 Corinthians 11:23-27 English Standard Version (ESV)

^{23} Are they servants of Christ? I am a better one—I am talking like a madman—with far greater labours, far more imprisonments, with countless beatings, and often near death. ^{24} Five times I received at the hands of the Jews the forty lashes less one. ^{25} Three times I was beaten with rods. Once I was stoned. Three times I was shipwrecked; a night and a day I was adrift at sea; ^{26} on frequent journeys, in danger from rivers, danger from robbers, danger from my own

people, danger from Gentiles, danger in the city, danger in the wilderness, danger at sea, danger from false brothers; [27] *in toil and hardship, through many a sleepless night, in hunger and thirst, often without food,*[a] *in cold and exposure.*

Then how about these people?

Polycarp

Polycarp was probably a disciple of the Apostle John. He may also have been one of the chief people responsible for compiling the New Testament of the Bible that we have today.

Because of his refusal to burn incense to the Roman Emperor he was sentenced to burn at the stake. Tradition says that the flames did not kill him so he was stabbed to death.

Wycliffe

John Wycliffe was a 14th century theologian. He believed that the Bible should be available to the people in their common language. He translated the Latin bible into common English.

He was persecuted for his stand against Papal authority. Wycliffe was not burned at the stake but his body was exhumed and burned along with many of his writings. The Anti-Wycliffe Statute of 1401 stated that there should not be any translation of

Scripture into English and resulted in the persecution of many of his followers (or more to the point Christs followers)

William Tyndale

William Tyndale is most famous as the original translators of the bible from its original language into common English which to this day still forms the majority of what is known as the King James Bible. He was also a reformer who stood against many teachings of the Catholic Church and opposed King Henry VIII's divorce, which was one of the major issues in the Reformation.

Tyndale was choked to <u>death</u> while tied to the stake and then his dead body was burned. The date of commemoration of Tyndale's martyrdom is October 6, 1536 but he probably died a few weeks earlier than that.

Dietrich Bonhoeffer

Pastor Dietrich Bonhoeffer was executed on June 9, 1945 because of his involvement in the July 20 Plot to kill Adolf Hitler. Bonhoeffer staunchly opposed Hitler's treatment of the Jews and was hanged just two weeks before soldiers from the United States liberated the concentration camp in which he was held.

(see also the story of the Oxford Martyrs in 1555 and check out the "Voice of Martyrs" website.

The Christian faith is not an invitation to a life of ease and comfort but a call to follow Christ and to do his will on earth that will enhance our relationship with him and draw people to him (not to ourselves or to our chosen place of worship but only to Christ.

There is more to this though let's take a look at some further reading.

Philippians 4:12 English Standard Version (ESV)

[12] I know how to be brought low, and I know how to abound. In any and every circumstance, I have learned the secret of facing plenty and hunger, abundance and need.

John 14:26 English Standard Version (ESV)

[26] But the Helper, the Holy Spirit, whom the Father will send in my name, he will teach you all things and bring to your remembrance all that I have said to you.

Psalm 46 English Standard Version (ESV)

God Is Our Fortress
To the choirmaster. Of the Sons of Korah. According to Alamoth.[a] A Song.
46 God is our refuge and strength, a

very present[b] help in trouble.
² Therefore we will not fear though the earth gives way, though the mountains be moved into the heart of the sea,
³ though its waters roar and foam, though the mountains tremble at its swelling. Selah

⁴ There is a river whose streams make glad the city of God, the holy habitation of the Most High.
⁵ God is in the midst of her; she shall not be moved; God will help her when morning dawns.
⁶ The nations rage, the kingdoms totter; he utters his voice, the earth melts.
⁷ The Lord of hosts is with us; the God of Jacob is our fortress. Selah

⁸ Come, behold the works of the Lord, how he has brought desolations on the earth.
⁹ He makes wars cease to the end of the earth; he breaks the bow and shatters the spear; he burns the chariots with fire
¹⁰ "Be still, and know that I am God. I will be exalted among the nations, I will be exalted in the earth!"
¹¹ The Lord of hosts is with us; the God of Jacob is our fortress. Selah

We will face trials and troubles in this life but God will be with us through them and will be our comfort throughout and will walk through those times with us.

Hebrews 6:17-20 English Standard Version (ESV)

[17] So when God desired to show more convincingly to the heirs of the promise the unchangeable character of his purpose, he guaranteed it with an oath, [18] so that by two unchangeable things, in which it is impossible for God to lie, we who have fled for refuge might have strong encouragement to hold fast to the hope set before us. [19] We have this as a sure and steadfast anchor of the soul, a hope that enters into the inner place behind the curtain, [20] where Jesus has gone as a forerunner on our behalf, having become a high priest forever after the order of Melchizedek.

As a Christian I can approach Christ in prayer at times of trouble and sometimes he will lift me from those troubles through miraculous changes of situations and other times he will lift me through the hope I have in him for the future and the knowledge that there is more to life than what I see day by day in the environment around me.

Bigots, Judges and the Self-righteous

There was a time when the biggest reason people refused to believe was because they did not want to be called a Christian due to the stuff they saw Christians doing and the attitudes they had towards other people. That remains a huge difficulty for us as we seek to make Christ known to others.

The first thing to say here is that we need to differentiate between Christ and Christians. Whether we are a good example of Christ or not we are all poor imitations of Christ. Christ is perfection. He has no pride, he has not prejudice and he will never betray our trust.

As hard as it is to admit, we as human beings will all make mistakes, we all consciously choose to sin and we all have prejudices based on our own past hurts and learnt behaviours. It is a fallacy when people claim to work, act or think in a non-judgemental way. We all make judgements. The best we can hope to do is to be part of a diverse group that challenges one another when our prejudices arise and be ready to listen and accept.

However there is much that the Church as an organisation and individuals within it have spoken and done in its name that causes people to turn their backs on Christ. Prior to becoming a Christian myself the biggest barrier I faced was in believing that there may indeed be a loving God but whenever I wanted to find out more I was met by people who defended "the church" rather than Christ.

When I eventually came across a person who was willing to accept that actually my long, long list of atrocities committed and stated by people who professed to be Christians was accurate and indefensible it made me take notice. He then put a bible in my hand and asked me to point out the places where such actions and statements were justified in the bible and in particular in the teachings of Christ.

He then showed me the opposite and where such behaviours were condemned by Christ. Certainly I could point to certain quotes often cited by Christians as instructions to bigotry which he would show me were actually being deliberately taken out of context. It really opened my eyes to something new.

There were things that challenged me and things I did not want to hear or accept about my own life. I was happy to see that all those things I disagreed with, Christ disagreed with too and that many things he taught I already agreed with but there was plenty that challenged me to think again about my views and attitudes. These though were not barriers.

However as I edged ever closer to taking the step of faith and after that there remained a barrier that still exists to this day. I have seen it damage the faith of so many people and it is about pride and a "holier than thou" issue.

A short while ago I heard a story of a Church leader returning late at night from a conference who arrived at a small service station. The only other vehicle in the car park was a minibus and emblazoned on the side was the name of a particular church. The pastor saw a group of people and after quite a long drive already approached them grateful for the opportunity to simply relax and spend time in the company of some other Christians.

He went over and asked them if they were with the minibus and if they attended the Church it belonged to. The group confirmed that yes indeed they were part of that church and he introduced himself. The leading voice asked him his denomination, that was acceptable, he asked him which particular branch of that denomination he was part of, that too was acceptable, he asked him how he felt about the gifts of the Holy Spirit and then in particular about the gift of tongues and then of healing. He asked him about predestination, Calvinism v Arminianism and so on.

Then he enquired about his views on the Eucharist/holy communion/lords supper and eventually found something on which they disagreed. At this point the leader and several people in the group rounded on the pastor explaining to him how he is deluded and a heretic etc.

When I heard this story the person telling it was telling it in an amusing way and was not particularly phased by the experience. He was however angered by what it represented which is exactly how some people behave. If we have chosen (or indeed been chosen) to follow Christ then we will meet similar people. We will be walking with Christ and someone somewhere will want to berate us and tell us that we are not fully saved or that we are in the wrong church or that in some way we are wet, judgemental, deluded or victims of a false gospel.

There is of course a problem here because there is a lot of false teaching out there and a lot of places where parts of the gospel are not fully accepted. How then are we to challenge false doctrine whilst at the same time avoiding condemnation and becoming smug in our own belief that we are right,

To be quite frank about it, it is a heart issue. I do not pretend to have everything sorted and neither do I expect anyone else to have all the right answers. There are some things that go directly against the teaching of the bible. God is love and as Peter says in the Bible:

2 Peter 3:8-10 English Standard Version (ESV)

[8] But do not overlook this one fact, beloved, that with the Lord one day is as a thousand years, and a thousand years as one day. [9] The Lord is not slow to fulfil his promise as some count slowness, but is patient toward you,[a] not wishing that any should perish, but that all should reach repentance. [10] But the day of the Lord will come like a thief, and then the heavens will pass away with a roar, and the heavenly bodies[b] will be burned up and dissolved, and the earth and the works that are done on it will be exposed.[c]

I am aware that I am very outspoken on the subject of the feel good get rich quick teachers and maybe at times I need to be careful about how that comes across to others. Unfortunately though I do see many people fall because they do not see this come to fruition in their lives. There are though other areas where I have views but cannot point to anything I see which confirms my views to be right or wrong. For example I hear many people argue, criticise and condemn on matters that will only be revealed at the end of our days.

These views include such areas as "Once saved – always saved", Predestination, singing in church, the use of a head covering and the appointing of teachers, pastors and elders.

Or issues around whether a Christian should listen to particular styles of music or what it is acceptable to watch and/or read. These should not be grounds for condemning but we should be able to discuss these and learn or agree to disagree without turning them into matters of division and schism.

Overall though this is really a short section to say that yes we are all faulty vessels of a perfect God. We all say and do silly things and we all carry the emotional scars of our past. We need to keep our focus on our relationship with Christ and not on our relationship with anything of the world.

In keeping our focus on Christ we do not become obnoxious in our dealings with others or dismissive of how our actions affect them but we become Christ like in the way we deal with others.

When we are facing people who seek to create division or condemn us for not agreeing with their view on matters of scripture we can listen and discuss and sometimes we may take stuff on board, at other times we may take something away to check out and at other times we will be able to simply disagree or see it as false. However never ever let it damage our faith and our relationship with Christ.

So Where is God When It Hurts and Why Does He Allow Suffering?

This is perhaps the hardest part of the Christians life. I nearly dismissed the subject as we have already touched on it but I think there is something far deeper to look at in this area.

There is a wonderful picture of Jesus talking with a young man and the young man asks him 2why do you allow so much suffering in the world?". Jesus responds by saying "Funny that – I was just about to ask you the same thing". More often than not the bog standard response to the questions at the top of this page is to say – because we have free will. That though is not enough.

Does the child have free will to choose terminal illness or abuse? Does the person trapped in a war zone or country enduring famine choose to be born and live in that time and place? Free will does not answer the question anywhere deeply enough.

There are some simple questions we can answer.

Much suffering is created by people. Wars, famine, most diseases and even the results of some natural disasters cause suffering. The world is fully stocked and resourced to meet the dietary and other needs of all its occupants but as a species we choose not to share them equally and those of us who do have access to the majority of the worlds resources waste them on throw away commodities. Consider that in 2004 1% of the world's population owned 45% of it resources and that 1% own more and more every year. There are countless opportunities for ordinary people to get involved and act to stop these kinds of events.

In many cases tyrannical governments are held up by the elected governments of the powerful west. Then when they go to war they kill and commit acts of genocide with weapons supplied by the west. In some of the recent worst atrocities this genocide has even been advocated through some of the teachings of the western missionaries competing for denominational convert numbers.

When we choose to ignore the political spectrum and allow wrong leaders on the basis that either we cannot be bothered or because we take it that when Paul say no authority will exist on earth without the will of God it is a call not to be part of the democratic process (by default handing the power over to anyone but us) we cannot then blame God for what those authorities choose to do. It is an act of their will and a result of our apathy. God doesn't cause war or allow it to happen we do.

Earthquake zones, volcanic sites and flood lands are known yet governments and businesses normally run by the top 0.05% know where these are but driven by greed create environments where they house masses of people against their wishes in these areas.

Famines caused by droughts in lands where crops are still being grown to export to pay off debts or because multinational companies have invested in those lands to maximise their own profits are also often the result of wasteful farming practice where the land has been stripped by the companies and then left waste as it is more profitable to move on to another site.

For many this is simply a case of us well fed, well-resourced people choosing greed over compassion and then throwing a few bits of shrapnel in some charity tin to make us feel a bit better. God is a convenient scapegoat we say why he lets it happen whilst ignoring our own role in making it happen or at best allowing it to happen.

I eat unhealthily, I smoke and I do very little exercise. On top of this I live in what may be called an industrial town. Should I go to the doctors and be told that I have high blood pressure, excessive body fat and respiratory problems I am not really in any position to blame God. Likewise for many people this goes for stress related illnesses and countless others.

However sometimes illness is not self-inflicted but a birth defect or a random event. I will come to these later but at the moment we can say that there are some illnesses that we inflict upon ourselves either directly through diet and habits or indirectly through that dread "G word" greed again to buy things we don't need for a budget price from unscrupulous businesses that pollute the air and water.

There are things we can do to alleviate a lot of suffering and choose not to. It is not this that I want to look at in this booklet, what I want to examine is where Christ is in personal pain that we can do little or nothing about.

All too often these days we read and hear of the suffering inflicted on people through the actions of others and whilst those who inflict pain are accountable for their actions it does not answer the question of WHY do some people suffer so much whilst others seem to live in relative luxury and ease.

Why does God allow the death of babies, the abuse of children and the victimisation and annihilation of cultures and races? Where is he for these people?

The role of free will

As I repeatedly say "God is Love" and everything has to be viewed from that viewpoint. Because God is love he does not and will not impose his will on anyone. He can only offer himself to them and they can choose to love or reject him. Because of this God is in a situation that is made impossible for him to win. If he imposes his will on anyone then he is controlling and tyrannical and his relationship with his people is abusive. Look at these three aspects of a controlling and coercive relationship –

- Choosing your family and friends for you and when you can see them.
- Controlling your money
- Monitoring your activities and movements

If God were to do these things for whatever reason then he would not be acting in love. Yes it may be to prevent us from choosing the wrong company, spending our money on the wrong things or getting involved in unproductive activities but it is controlling us rather than letting choose to love him. Sadly for us we do not live in a bubble of isolation and therefore our actions affect others.

I have often wondered about sickness and disease. I have always been around household pets and can list the illnesses they get very quickly. When it comes to human beings the list of possible sicknesses and diseases gets longer and longer by the day almost. As I pondered on this point it occurred to me that for too long the stock answer has been that humans are corrupted through sin and therefore sickness and disease entered them.

Is this just another of those rubbish cliché answers?

What does it mean?

We were created perfect and in the image of God. Everything God created was perfect and created for its purpose. There are products created to eat, products created to heal, product created for aesthetic beauty, products created to build and products created to cleanse. As a species we reproduce by passing on stuff produced in our own bodies to stuff produced in someone else's body to combine and create another life. That is putting it in simple terms.

It is basic and obvious however that what we put into our bodies influences what we produce. Therefore if everything God created is perfect for its purpose then surely our physical bodies should remain perfected if we put in only what is created for that purpose and treat them in accordance with the purpose for which they were created. Having always had pets and having spent a lot of time around animals something that I have observed is that for the most part animals are very picky about what they will and will not eat. I can put down a bowl of food for cats and dogs and they wolf down everything but leave one or two bits in the bottom or will sniff a plate and walk away.

The exception to this tends to be goats and pigs that will eat everything and anything regardless of what it is. The reasoning for the majority of animals is that they can sense normally by smell if there is something not right with the food put in front of them. Human beings on the other hand will knowingly and willingly poison themselves for entertainment and amusement.

I am not a puritan and would not label myself as teetotal but whilst it is commonly stated that the most common source of food poisoning is dairy products, out of date meats and seafood this is not strictly true. They are sources of involuntary food poisoning. Alcohol is consumed voluntarily because of the effects on the body which are by definition food poisoning. Alcohol used medicinally may cleanse wounds and kill bacteria, when it enters the body though its effects are different.

It causes certain body functions to shut down as the body identifies a toxin and seeks to remove it. This is what causes the sensation of drunkenness. Human beings knowingly use alcohol, tobacco, caffeine and other substances to deliberately poison their bodies because they enjoy the effects. Likewise there are foods that are unhealthy but taste nice. On top of all this there are the products that are pumped into the air that we create and the chemicals we add to foods. When our bodies tell us to rest so they can heal properly we pump ourselves full of analgesics to speed up the process or to mask the pain so that we can carry on.

So we do not allow our bodies to heal fully in the manner they were created to heal, we pump the air full of toxins which we breathe in and we deliberately poison ourselves for entertainment and pleasure and then we blame God for sickness and disease. There is no polite way really of putting this but when we ask about children who are born sick we need consider whether this God allowing it or the result of generation after generation poisoning their bodies.

This is not about blaming anyone and definitely not blaming the parents. I am simply asking whether or not we should consider the fact that we poison ourselves and then expect that not to affect the fruit we produce and that could be many generations later.

God could dictate and control us like robots, he could surround us with a protective wall but he gives us wisdom and gives us choice. We blame him for the results of human choices.

How about the innocent victims though, how about those who have no choice in the effects of the sins and actions of others? Surely a loving God could protect them until they are old enough or wise enough to choose? This is such a tough question and one that we have to be sensitive about. It would be easy to turn around and say that God gives us responsibility to look out for the innocent and vulnerable and that is absolutely correct.

However once again we look for someone to blame when that fails. When a family member or family friend mistreats or abuses a child is it Gods fault, the parents fault, societies fault or the abusers fault alone? God is easy to blame because he is love and he should have protected that child. We know though that this stuff goes on and it is the hardest area to understand or believe there can possibly be a God in a world where it goes on.

Sadly there are no easy answers and there are none that cannot be interpreted as blaming anyone other than the abuser. You will know the stuff – who allowed it to go on, who failed to protect the victim? When a child dies there is always a serious case review and someone's head is going to roll as a result of a lack of protection. Blaming God is part of the same thinking, it is seeking to blame someone other than the perpetrator for the crime (sin). There is something though to be said about a society that creates people who do this sort of thing, whether that is a parent who neglects, humiliates or beats a child or a predator who seeks out a child to abuse. This is a society problem.

It is not a case though that society should absolve the guilty of blame. Popular and underground society create a culture where lines are blurred and morality deliberately pushed to and at times beyond its boundaries often for the same reason people physically poison themselves – entertainment.

Films can have an 18 certificate or have a warning on the front about explicit content but it is more an advertisement than a warning. We poison our bodies and our minds and subsequently our spirits and then blame God for the consequences.

I could go on and on about this subject but let's just look at the end question. Where is God in all this?

God is there healing the broken.

Christ's first teaching engagement says:

Luke 4:16-30 English Standard Version (ESV)

Jesus Rejected at Nazareth
[16] And he came to Nazareth, where he had been

brought up. And as was his custom, he went to the synagogue on the Sabbath day, and he stood up to read. [17] And the scroll of the prophet Isaiah was given to him. He unrolled the scroll and found the place where it was written,
[18] "The Spirit of the Lord is upon me, because he has anointed me to proclaim good news to the poor. He has sent me to proclaim liberty to the captives and recovering of sight to the blind, to set at liberty those who are oppressed,
[19] to proclaim the year of the Lord's favor."

[20] And he rolled up the scroll and gave it back to the attendant and sat down. And the eyes of all in the synagogue were fixed on him. [21] And he began to say to them, "Today this Scripture has been fulfilled in your hearing." [22] And all spoke well of him and marveled at the gracious words that were coming from his mouth. And they said, "Is not this Joseph's son?" [23] And he said to them, "Doubtless you will quote to me this proverb, 'Physician, heal yourself.' What we have heard you did at Capernaum, do here in your hometown as well.'"

[24] And he said, "Truly, I say to you, no prophet is acceptable in his hometown. [25] But in truth, I tell you, there were many widows in Israel in the days of Elijah, when the heavens were shut up three years and six months, and a great famine came over all the land, [26] and Elijah was sent to none of them but only to Zarephath, in the land of Sidon, to a woman who was a widow. [27] And there were

many lepers[a] in Israel in the time of the prophet Elisha, and none of them was cleansed, but only Naaman the Syrian." ²⁸ When they heard these things, all in the synagogue were filled with wrath. ²⁹ And they rose up and drove him out of the town and brought him to the brow of the hill on which their town was built, so that they could throw him down the cliff. ³⁰ But passing through their midst, he went away.

This is Christ. He heals and restores the broken.

Joel 2:23-28 English Standard Version (ESV)

²³ "Be glad, O children of Zion, and rejoice in the Lord your God, for he has given the early rain for your vindication; he has poured down for you abundant rain, the early and the latter rain, as before.
²⁴ "The threshing floors shall be full of grain; the vats shall overflow with wine and oil.
²⁵ I will restore[a] to you the years that the swarming locust has eaten, the hopper, the destroyer, and the cutter, my great army, which I sent among you.
²⁶ "You shall eat in plenty and be satisfied, and praise the name of the Lord your God, who has dealt wondrously with you. And my people shall never again be put to shame.
²⁷ You shall know that I am in the midst of Israel, and that I am the Lord your God and there is none else. And my people shall never again be put to shame.

The Lord Will Pour Out His Spirit
28 [b] "And it shall come to pass afterward, that I will pour out my Spirit on all flesh; your sons and your daughters shall prophesy, your old men shall dream dreams, and your young men shall see visions.

Peter quotes this reference in the very first sermon ever preached following Pentecost and right before we are instructed on the role of the church.

Because we have free will God needs an invitation to come and heal our brokenness.

Next Steps

So what do we do now?

Our faith is not static, we do not become a Christian and say that's it. I have mentioned many times the frustration I feel when people share a testimony that ends with "and then I got saved". Some people have been giving the same story for years and years. However Jesus is constantly at work in our lives. He expects us to grow. Look at this reading.

Hebrews 5:12-14 English Standard Version (ESV)

12 For though by this time you ought to be teachers, you need someone to teach you again the basic principles of the oracles of God. You need milk, not solid food, 13 for everyone who lives on milk is unskilled in the word of righteousness, since he is a child. 14 But solid food is for the mature, for those who have their powers of discernment trained by constant practice to distinguish good from evil.

We need to continue to learn and then to pass that learning on. Do not keep this amazing gift to yourself. It is something to share. If you have been saved for ten minutes you already have ten minutes more to share than you did ten minutes ago. Tell people what you have learnt and what Christ is doing in your life. We read the following -

Acts 17:11 English Standard Version (ESV)

11 Now these Jews were more noble than those in Thessalonica; they received the word with all eagerness, examining the Scriptures daily to see if these things were so.

What I have been grabbed by recently is the wording here. "They received the word with all eagerness." Lets eagerly receive teaching, test it against scripture and then shared what they learnt.

- Fellowship,
- Learn,
- Serve,
- Share.

Wrap this up in prayer and we are on the right path for growth and a faith that moves ourselves and others.

About the Author

Neville Wheeler has over thirty years of experience in helping people to overcome life-controlling problems which include addictions and compulsive behaviours.

The majority of this work has been within the YMCA in the UK, but he has also served people in voluntary and statutory youth services, adult substance misuse rehabilitation projects and secular supported housing projects.

During that time, Neville has served thousands of people and has worked with a variety of recovery programmes and models, seeing how each one works for different people.

He has worked at all levels, ranging from volunteering to project management. It is clear that Neville's passion and skill lie in face-to face work rather than the board room politics of stakeholders meetings, funding bids and competition.

Born in the county of Essex, England, and raised mostly on the south coast of Dorset. Neville spent his teenage years in the 1980s mixed up in the anger and rebellion that came along with the punk scene at that time. He finally accepted Christ as his Saviour in 1986. Work has seen him move around the country having lived and worked in the South, the Midlands and the North West.

This has also given him a wide view of programmes and how they work as well as different churches and common barriers and helps that exist in the church for those labelled as socially excluded.

As a Christian first and foremost, Neville is passionate to see people come to know Jesus Christ as their Lord and Saviour. After a somewhat cynical approach to Christ-centred Support and Recovery Programmes, he has become convinced that the Gospel is what so many people are calling out for.

In response to this need, he has developed a number of training programmes for those wishing to work in this area and projects to bring the Gospel to people in a non-invasive way whilst never shying away from difficult subject matters.

Neville currently lives in South Wales with his wife Nora and where his grown up children and their families also live.

As life moves on, he is keen now to pass on the benefits of his many years of experience including the good, the bad and the ugly…so that as many lives as possible can be changed through what he has learnt.

Neville is available for training events and speaking engagements to share his wealth of experience and training for those who wish to bring the gospel to those in need.

If you would like to either arrange or book an event, he can be reached by email:

maplit2018@gmail.com

Printed in Poland
by Amazon Fulfillment
Poland Sp. z o.o., Wrocław